CREEPY CRAWLERS

P Phidal

Part 1

Match each slimy creature with its home.

Complete the sets and add up the pesky little bugs.

Place the scary insects on their shadows to complete each pattern.

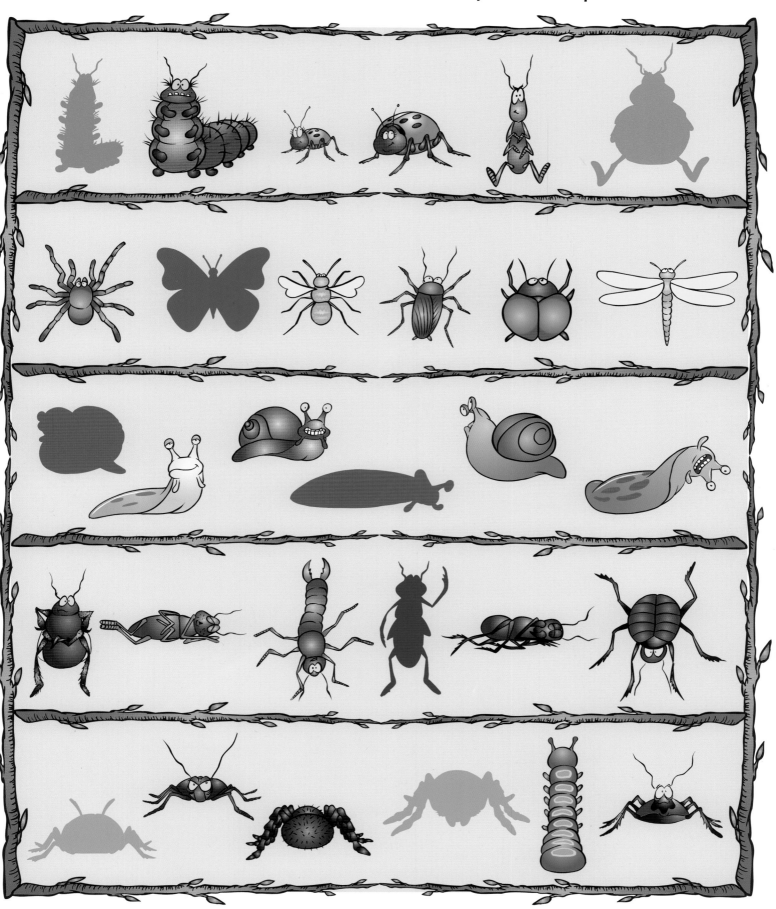

5

Decorate the scene and discover the tiny world of bugs.

Add or subtract the silly crawlers to find the right answer.

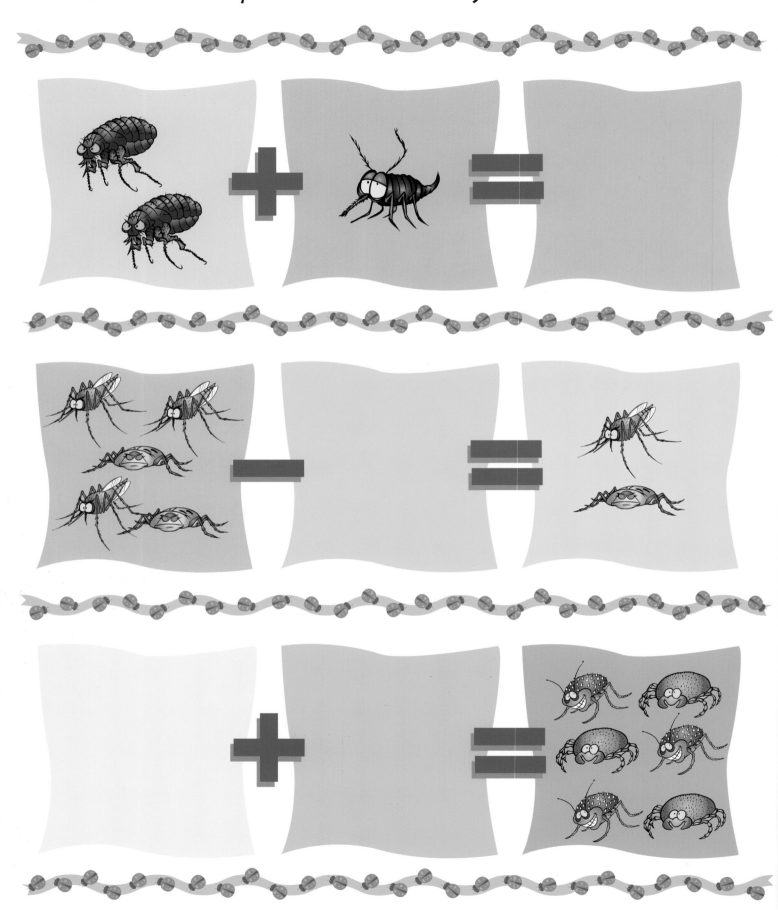

Complete the scene by placing each weird bug on its shadow.

Place the creepy insects in the squares and answer the questions:

Who has colorful wings?

Who hops?

Who stings?

Who buzzes?

Who moves very slowly?

Who spins a web?

Who makes music at night?

Who loves to eat leaves?

Place these nasty critters in order, from the least to the most number of legs.

CRAZY ANIMALS

Part

II

Place each crazy animal beside the right shape.

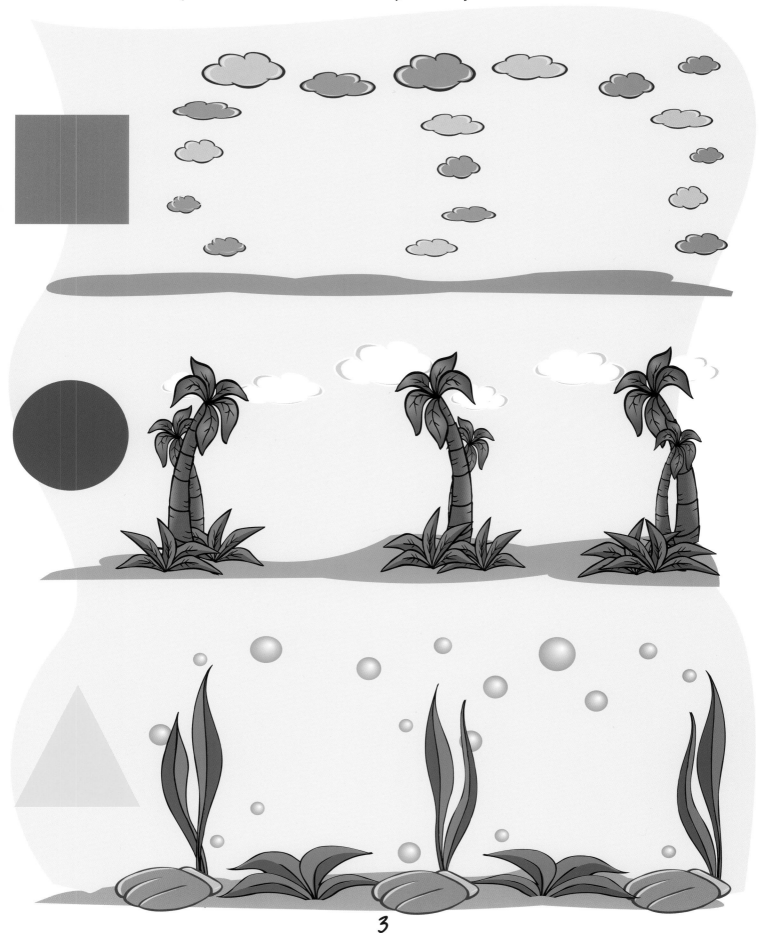

Complete every set with the strange beasts missing.

Who eats what?

Decorate the scene and let your imagination run wild.

Complete the bottom image with the odd predators missing.

Complete the scene by placing each scary animal on its shadow.

Add up the silly animals to complete the table.

Find the surprising opposite of each animal.

Big   Small

Fat   Thin

Top   Bottom

Angry   Happy

Fast   Slow

ALIENS

Phidal

PART III

Match each galactic pilot with his spaceship.

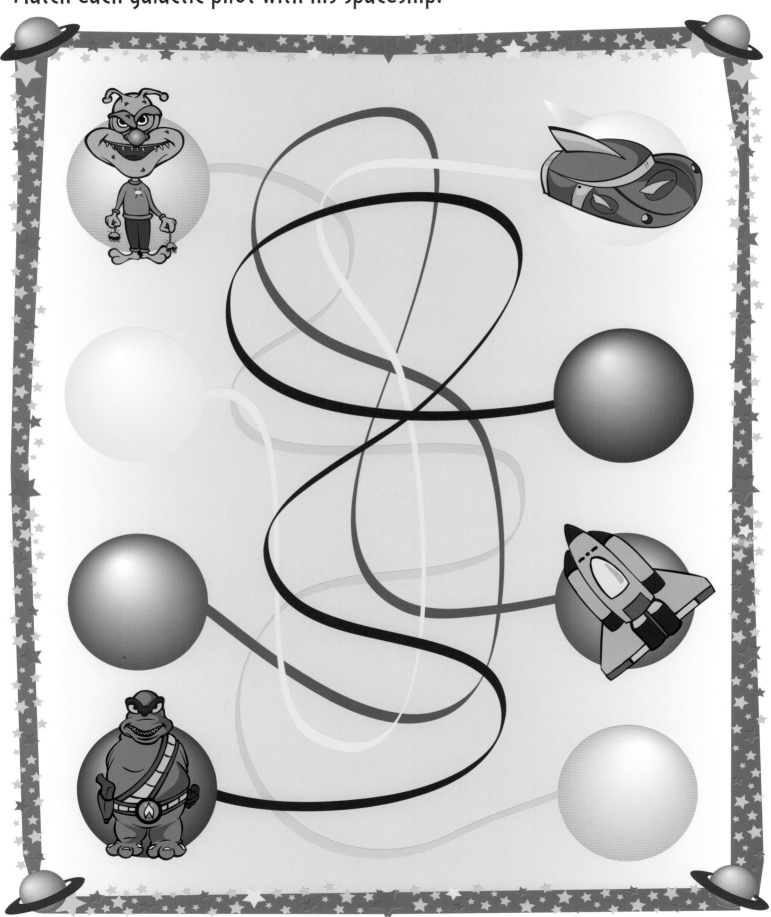

Join in the cosmic war by placing each sticker on the right shape.

5

Decorate the scene and invade an exciting new planet.

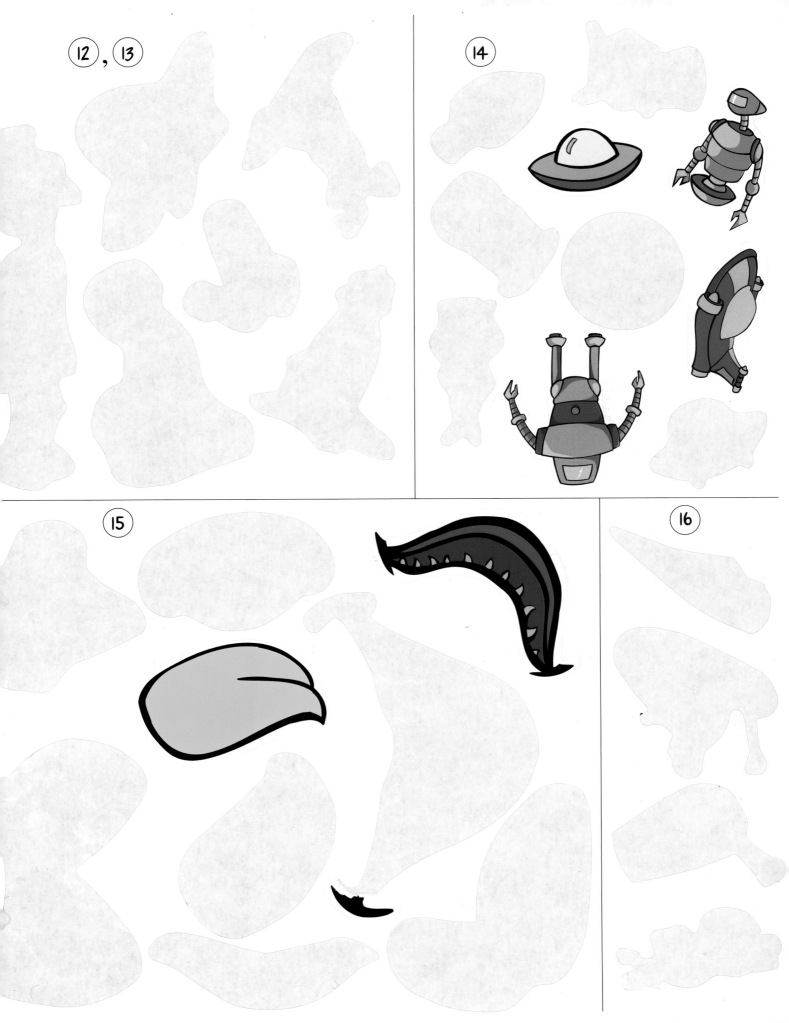

12 , 13

14

15

16

Find each alien's weird opposite.

Standing

Far

Sitting

Weak

Strong

Short

Over

Under

Happy

Tall

Sad

Complete these sets from outer space and add them up.

Spaceships

7

Aliens

6

Planets

3

Robots

4

14

Use your stickers to create the wackiest alien.

Find the strange objects hidden in the scene.

DEEP-SEA MONSTERS

Phidal

Part

IV

Use the shapes to group and sort these prickly fish.

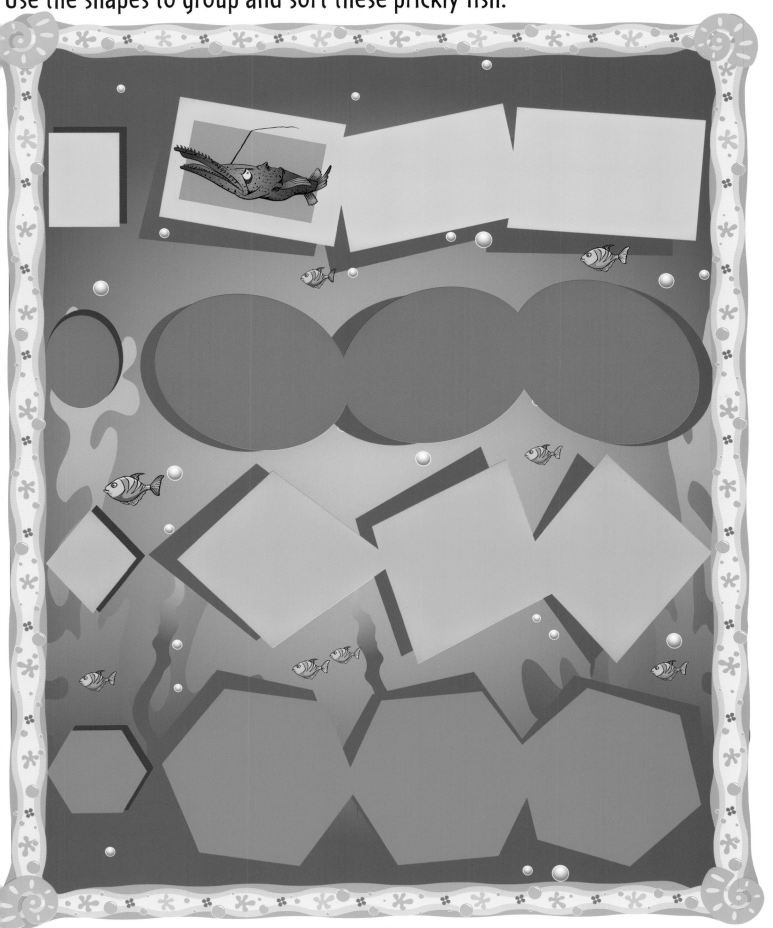

Hide the slimy creatures in the background.

Decorate the scene and enter the unknowns of the deep sea.

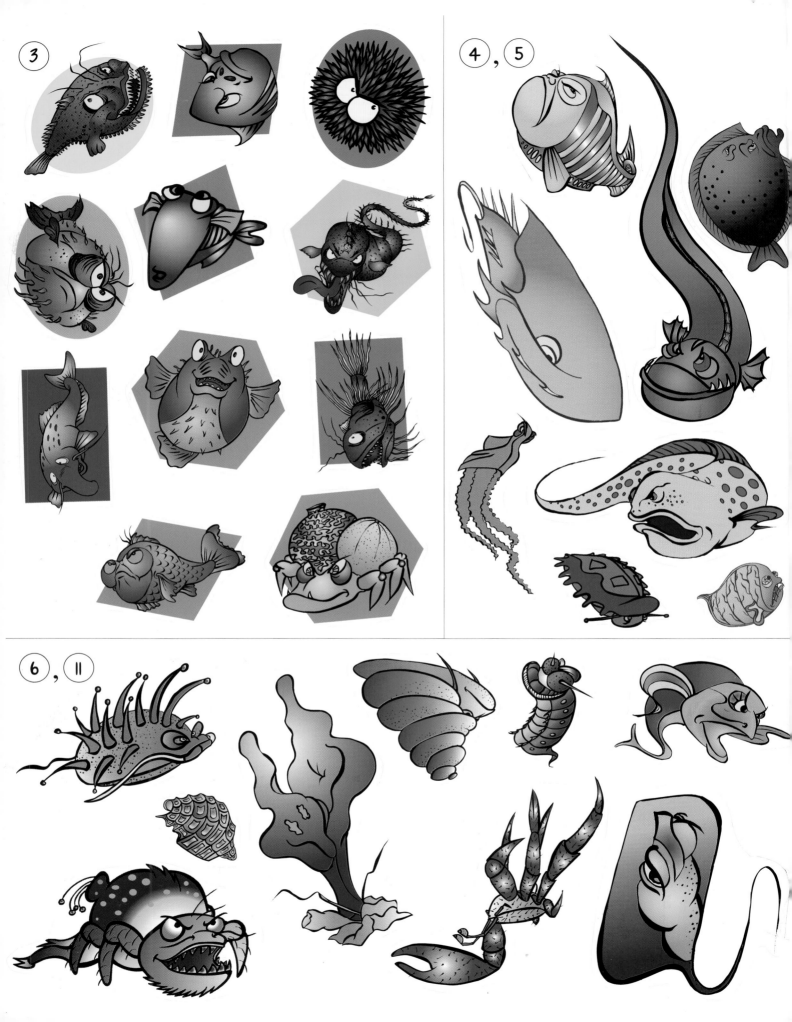

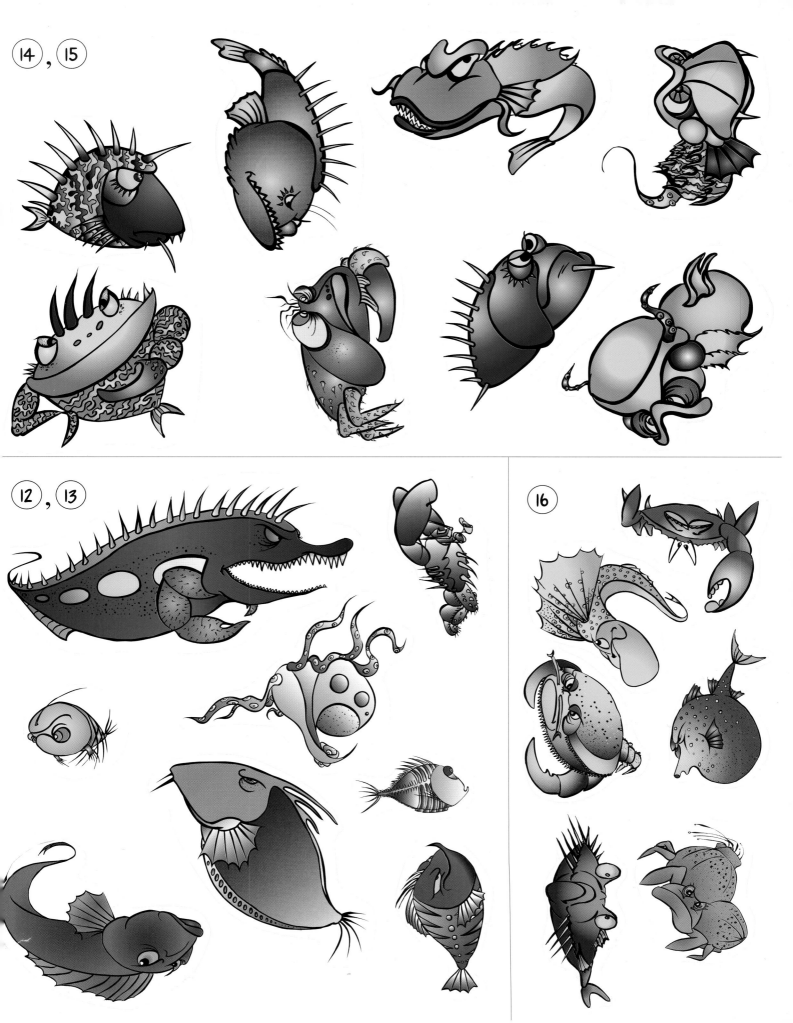

Follow the arrows and complete this food chain.

Cross the fish on the left with the fish at the top, to create wacky animals.

Sort these strange underwater creatures by color.